THIS BOOK BELONGS TO:

_____

The Wonderful World of Piping Plovers

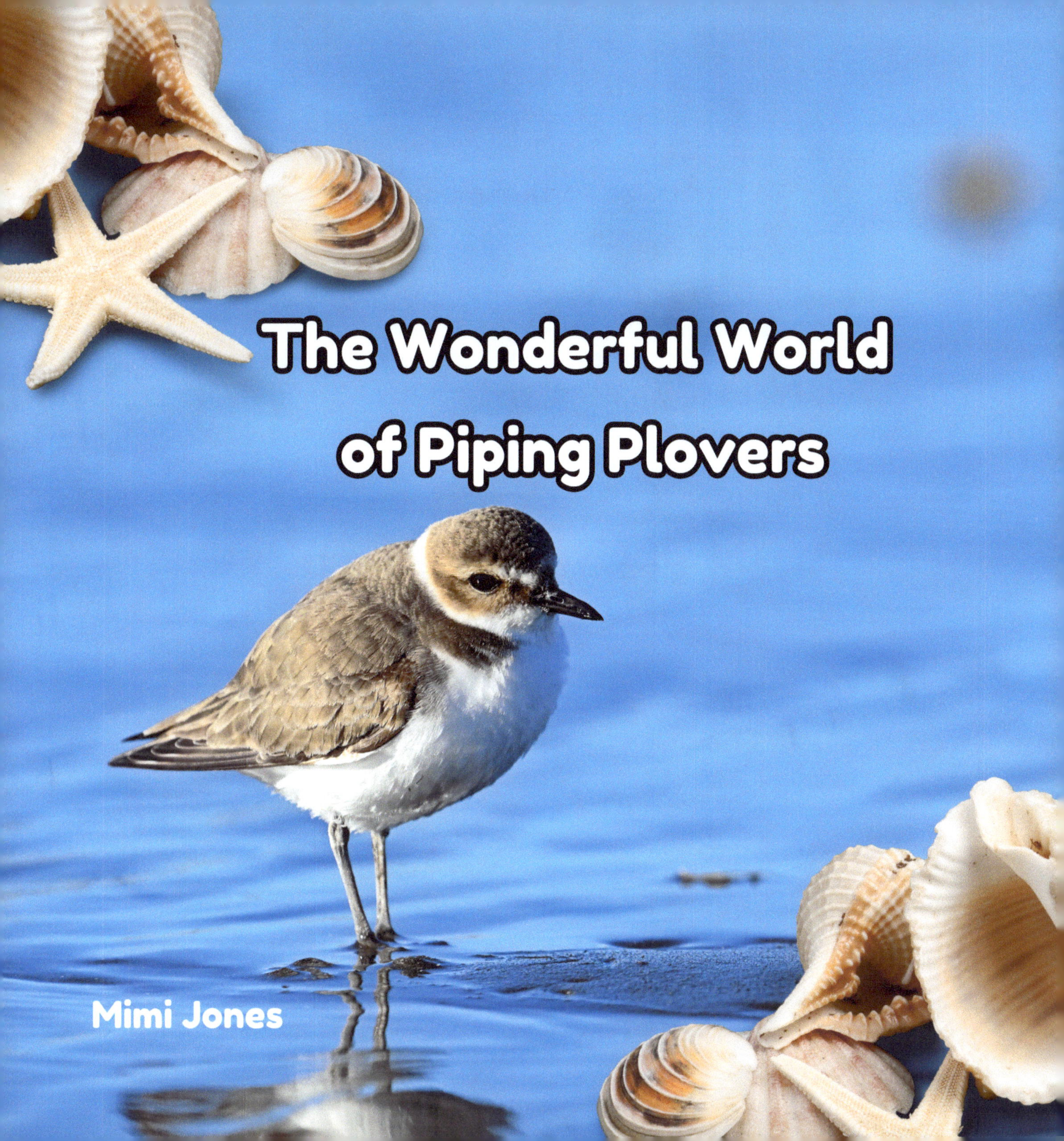

Mimi Jones

Dedicated to all the bird lovers.

ISBN 978-1-958985-38-0

www.joeysavestheday.com

A Mimi Book

Welcome to the Wonderful World of Piping Plovers

Piping plovers are small shorebirds with a distinctive sand-colored plumage, which helps them blend into their beach habitat.

These birds are named for their melodic, piping calls that are often heard during the breeding season.

Piping plovers have a black band across their foreheads and a black ring around their necks, most noticeable during the breeding season. They have bright orange legs and a short, stubby bill that is also orange with a black tip.

During courtship, male piping plovers perform elaborate displays that include skimming along the sand and calling to potential mates.

Both parents take turns incubating the eggs, which helps ensure the eggs are kept warm and protected. The incubation period for piping plover eggs lasts about 25-30 days, after which the chicks hatch. Piping plovers use a "broken-wing" display to distract predators away from their nests and chicks.

Piping plovers typically lay three to four eggs per clutch, which are camouflaged to blend in with the sandy surroundings. The chicks develop their feathers within 25-35 days of hatching, allowing them to fly and escape predators.

Piping plover chicks are precocial, meaning they can walk and feed themselves shortly after hatching.

Piping plovers are excellent at camouflaging themselves against the sandy beach, making them difficult to spot.

Their preferred habitats include sandy beaches, sandbars, and shorelines where they can nest and forage.

Piping plovers are carnivores. Their diet consists mainly of insects, marine worms, and small crustaceans, which they find by probing the sand with their beaks.

They have a lifespan of about five years in the wild, although some individuals can live longer.

ENDANGERED SPECIES !

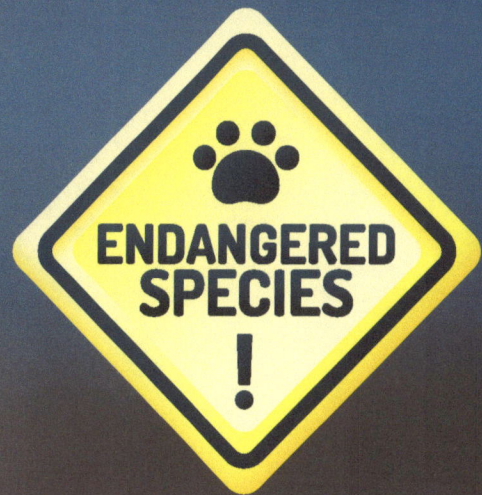

Piping plovers are listed as endangered and threatened in many regions due to habitat loss and human disturbance. Conservation efforts for piping plovers include habitat protection, management, and monitoring programs.

Piping plovers are native to North America. Piping plover populations are divided into three distinct groups: Atlantic Coast, Great Lakes, and Northern Great Plains. The Atlantic Coast population is the largest of the three groups.

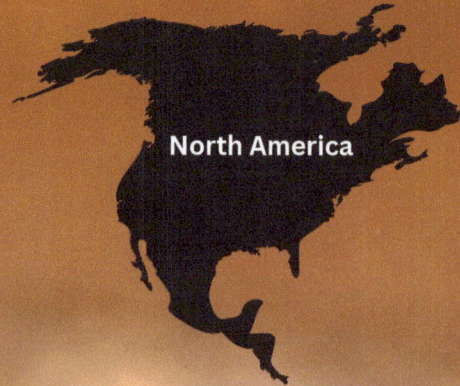

North America

Survive

Wildlife agencies and conservation groups often monitor and protect piping plover nesting areas to ensure their survival.

Banding is a standard method used to track piping plovers and gather data on their movements and populations.

In some regions, artificial nesting habitats are created to support and boost piping plover populations.

These birds are migratory, spending the winter months in the southern United States, the Caribbean, and along the Gulf Coast.

Piping plovers play an important role in their ecosystem by helping to control insect populations.

Piping plovers are primarily diurnal. They are most active during the day, especially during the early morning and late afternoon when they forage for food.

Their scientific name is Charadrius melodus, which reflects their melodious calls.

Symbolic fencing is often used to protect piping plover nesting areas from human disturbance and predators.

CAUTION   CAUTION   CAUTION

They frequently revisit the same nesting locations annually, demonstrating a strong attachment to these sites.

They are a popular subject for birdwatchers and photographers due to their unique appearance and behaviors.

Piping plovers are recognized as indicator species, which means that their presence serves as a reflection of the health of their habitat and ecosystem.

WAY TO

BEACH

If not managed effectively, dogs and other pets can present serious threats to the nests and chicks of piping plovers. Additionally, human recreational activities on beaches—such as walking, driving, and playing—can disrupt these vulnerable nests and their young.

Piping plovers are often involved in habitat restoration projects that aim to restore and protect their critical nesting and foraging areas.

Count the Piping Plovers.

THE END!

www.ingramcontent.com/pod-product-compliance
Lightning Source LLC
Chambersburg PA
CBHW041346290326
41933CB00036B/131